Connecting Cultures Through Family and Food

The Greek Family Table

by Diane Bailey

The Greek Family Table

By Diane Bailey

MASON CREST

Mason Crest
450 Parkway Drive, Suite D
Broomall, PA 19008
www.masoncrest.com

Printed and bound in the United States of America.

Series ISBN: 978-1-4222-4041-0
Hardback ISBN: 978-1-4222-4044-1
EBook ISBN: 978-1-4222-7742-3

First printing
9 8 7 6 5 4 3 2 1

Produced by Shoreline Publishing Group LLC
Santa Barbara, California
Editorial Director: James Buckley Jr.
Designer: Tom Carling
Production: Patty Kelley
www.shorelinepublishing.com

Front cover: Piksel/Dreamstime.com (top); Boris Kotov/Shutterstock (bottom).

Library of Congress Cataloging-in-Publication Data
Names: Bailey, Diane, 1966- author. Title: The Greek family table / by Diane Bailey.
Description: Broomall, PA : Mason Crest, 2018. | Series: Connecting cultures through family and food | Includes bibliographical references and index.
Identifiers: LCCN 2017053426| ISBN 9781422240441 (hardback) | ISBN 9781422240410 (series) | ISBN 9781422277423 (ebook)
Subjects: LCSH: Cooking, Greek--Juvenile literature. | Food habits--Greece--Juvenile literature. | Greek Americans--Food--Juvenile literature. | United States--Emigration and immigration--Juvenile literature. | Greece--Social life and customs--Juvenile literature.
Classification: LCC TX723.5.G8 B255 2018 | DDC 641.59495--dc23 LC record available at https://lccn.loc.gov/2017053426

QR Codes disclaimer:

Contents

KEY ICONS TO LOOK FOR

Words to Understand: These words with their easy-to-understand definitions will increase the reader's understanding of the text, while building vocabulary skills.

Sidebars: This boxed material within the main text allows readers to build knowledge, gain insights, explore possibilities, and broaden their perspectives by weaving together additional information to provide realistic and holistic perspectives.

Educational Videos: Readers can view videos by scanning our QR codes, providing them with additional educational content to supplement the text. Examples include news coverage, moments in history, speeches, iconic moments, and much more!

Text-Dependent Questions: These questions send the reader back to the text for more careful attention to the evidence presented here.

Research Projects: Readers are pointed toward areas of further inquiry connected to each chapter. Suggestions are provided for projects that encourage deeper research and analysis.

Series Glossary of Key Terms: This back-of-the-book glossary contains terminology used throughout this series. Words found here increase the reader's ability to read and comprehend higher-level books and articles in this field.

Introduction
Home at the Table

Maybe it's not surprising that, for centuries, many Greeks never left their homeland. Traveling abroad was difficult, since the country's mainland is mostly bordered by the sea. Famous legends told of Greek sailors who explored distant lands, but that wasn't a way of life for most. Trekking through the mountainous interior was also time-consuming and treacherous, especially before mechanized vehicles entered the picture. Offshore, the smattering of islands that freckles the Mediterranean, Aegean, and Ionian seas was home to people who were even more isolated.

Still, there was little reason to leave. Greece is one of the oldest developed civilizations in the world. It's famous for being the birthplace of democracy. The weather's pretty good too, with gentle sea breezes and the warm climate of the Mediterranean. People caught a bounty of fish and other seafood from the ocean. Inland, goats and sheep roamed the rocky mountains. And although the land isn't particularly good for farming, people were able to raise some important crops, such as olives and grapes.

Eventually people did venture out, though. When Greece faced hard times, people were forced to leave in search of a better life. They didn't take much with them. They packed some clothes, a little money, and maybe a family photograph. But they also brought something that didn't take up any room in their suitcase: their culture. They had music, folk dances,

and special ways of celebrating holidays. And of course, they had food. Sharing meals with family, friends, and even strangers was a way of life in Greece. And when Greeks went to their new countries, it was an important way to bring their old lives with them even as they started new ones. As an old Greek saying goes, "If the pot boils, friendship lives."

Getting Here

When Hrisanthi Androutsos sailed through New York Harbor in the early 1920s and saw the famous Statue of Liberty on Ellis Island, she was excited to start a new life. At 24, she'd agreed to come to America to be married—to a husband she'd never even met! She was one of thousands who followed the same path. Some of them were nervous about their new life, but Hrisanthi was excited about her future in the United States. Despite not knowing how to speak English, she was smart and educated. She'd helped in a family store back in Greece, and she knew she could help her husband with the store he was running in Los Angeles.

Her future husband was a Greek immigrant who had already settled in the United States. A few months earlier, he had sent word back to Greece that he needed a wife.

Words to Understand

capitalize take advantage of; build upon

diaspora a large migration of a specific culture or people

self-sufficient able to survive without outside help

supply chain a series of businesses that trades goods to reach markets

In the early 1900s, when Greek immigration to the United States and Canada began to grow, Greece itself still had a largely agrarian and fishing economy.

The two exchanged photographs, and Hrisanthi came over as a "picture bride." With her, she brought her intelligence, her determination, and her memories. She was leaving Greece, but she was not leaving behind all that her country meant to her. That she would bring with her.

A Modern World

By the second half of the nineteenth century, the Second Industrial Revolution was well underway throughout the world. This period lasted roughly a century, beginning in 1850, and peaking from about 1870 to 1920.

In the past, most people had lived in rural areas or small towns. Cities were much smaller than they are today. The majority of people worked at jobs that used the resources of the land, such as agriculture or logging. Most communities were largely **self-sufficient**. They might order luxury goods such as fancy cloth from distant places, but they could survive on what they could make and grow.

The Second Industrial Revolution changed all that. Technology was ad-

Greeks in Egypt

America was the big draw for most Greek immigrants, but it was not the only one. In the 1800s, the country of Egypt began recruiting all kinds of immigrants to come to the country and improve it. The British were put in charge of the military and police; the French took care of the ports; the Italians were brought in as architects; and the Greeks were recruited for their skills in agriculture. By the mid-1800s, the American cotton market was in trouble because of turmoil from the Civil War. Fighting disrupted **supply chains**, and after the war, the abolition of slavery meant the end of a huge, free labor market for plantation owners. Greeks in Egypt took advantage of this to build the Egyptian cotton market into an international powerhouse.

The industrialization that spread across Europe and America created great upheaval in the economy, but also created many factory jobs.

vancing rapidly. It had started decades earlier, with the invention of the steam engine, but now even more powerful and sophisticated machinery dominated.

Textile mills and steel factories started to produce large quantities of goods. Electricity became widespread. Telephones and automobiles were invented. The Industrial Revolution did not affect all countries the same. African and Asian nations, as well as some European nations such as Greece and Italy, were not able to fully **capitalize** on the technological advances. But others, including Canada, Britain, Australia, and especially the United States, were transforming their economies.

Factories and mills required huge numbers of workers. Many of the jobs were not particularly difficult. They were repetitive and did not require much skill. They did not pay very much, either. But there were a lot of them, more than could be filled by native populations. Immigrants could help satisfy the demand.

Trouble in Greece

A few thousand emigrants had left Greece in the 1870s and 1880s. Then, in the 1890s, Greece faced a crisis. Its economy was narrow and fragile. The country's main export was currants, a dried berry similar to a raisin grape. France was the main buyer, but then the French government put a high tax on Greek currants so French people would instead buy those that were grown in France. The bottom fell out of the Greek currant

A crash in the Greek currant market was one reason immigration began to expand.

Greek history in Chicago

market. When the price tanked, so did Greece's economy. Many Greeks found themselves bankrupt, unable to pay their taxes or make a living.

They knew there were jobs in other countries, though. Desperate to try to make it somewhere else, emigrants began leaving Greece in even bigger numbers than they had in the last two decades. Most of them came from the Greek mainland or the Peloponnese, a peninsula connected to the southern part of the country, but some also came from the Greek islands and Asia Minor (modern-day Turkey).

The Greek **diaspora**—Greeks living abroad—spread all over the world, but for many, the United States was the land of opportunity. Between 1890 and the early 1920s, about 400,000 Greeks settled throughout the country. Many lived in cities in the Northeast and Midwest, such as New York, Chicago, and Detroit. Some went to the West, and a few settled in the South. In each region, they led slightly different lives. In the Northeast, many jobs were in the textile mills. The West offered employment in mines and building the railroad. Agriculture was a dominant industry in the South. And all over, Greeks (especially younger boys) found work as street vendors, selling fruit and candy, and shining shoes.

At first, the vast majority of Greek immigrants were men, since the job market demanded manual laborers. Some had relatives to help them, but many others depended on *padrones*, who served as labor brokers. Often these were fellow Greeks who were already established, and promised to help new immigrants find jobs. Unfortunately, this system was corrupt, and padrones would charge high fees. The jobs were low-paying and sometimes fell through soon after they had started.

When they did get a job, working twelve-hour days or longer, these men had little time for fun, and little money for luxuries. To save money on rent, they often shared quarters in boardinghouses. Sometimes one man was designated to take care of the home chores, such as cleaning, shopping, and cooking. Not that they were eating anything very fancy! One early menu went like this: "Monday: rice and wieners; Tuesday: potatoes and wieners; Wednesday: eggs and wieners; Thursday: lentils and wieners; Friday: greens and wieners; Saturday: beans in cottonseed oil; Sunday: meat, soup, and beer."

There wasn't a lot of variety, but it was simple, nutritious food, and that was enough. Peggy Glowacki, a historian who curated a 2007 museum exhibit about the influence of food on Greek immigrants to Chicago, notes, "For the first couple of decades the Greek immigrants just wanted to make enough money to go back home and make a better life for their families. So they re-created the frugal meals they ate in Greece, and these familiar foods were also an emotional link to their loved ones."

Ebb and Flow

In 1924, the United States changed its laws to severely limit the number of immigrants who were allowed to enter the country. Part of the reason was that the Industrial Revolution had mostly run its course. There was not a need for nearly as many workers. But a bigger reason was a growing anti-immigrant sentiment. With so many foreigners coming to America, native citizens began to feel threatened. The boatloads of immigrants coming through Ellis Island in New York Harbor were no longer a familiar sight, and this was the case for the next 40 years.

The laws were again changed in 1965 and the restrictions were loosened. A new wave of Greek immigrants began to arrive in the 1960s and 1970s. These new immigrants were different from their predecessors. The

The entry point for millions of immigrants, Ellis Island is today a National Historic Park and a popular tourist destination.

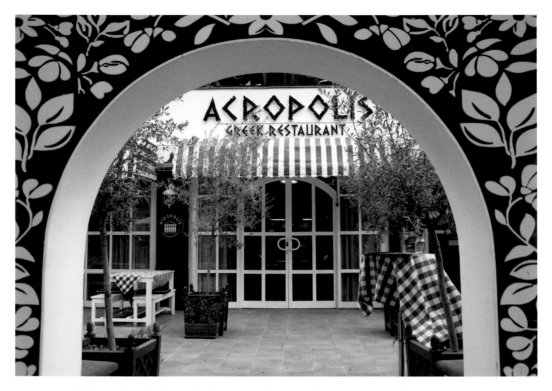

When Greeks found their new homes, they were quick to open restaurants to make sure they could enjoy the food of home.

original immigrants were mostly poor or working-class people hoping to live the "American Dream" and make a better life for their children. Like other immigrants, they took whatever jobs they could find, good or bad. Long hours, dangerous working conditions, and low pay were all common factors in their lives, but they were willing to make the sacrifice to provide for their families and build a future.

In contrast, later immigrants were often already well educated. They were doctors and lawyers, architects and engineers. They went to America, Europe, and the United Kingdom hoping to use the skills they'd already acquired, or to study abroad.

The problems faced by new immigrants were not as dramatic as those faced by earlier ones. Rather than worrying about *how* to put food on the table, they worried more about what *kind* of food it was. "I found myself constantly hungry and dissatisfied with dorm food," remembers Carol Malakasis, who came to the U.S. in the early 2000s to attend school. All the takeout, potato chips, and ramen noodles in the world would not cure my cranky hunger. Instead of celebrating my 'freedom'" away from my small hometown of Preveza, I could not wait for winter break to go home to mom, where I would be greeted with my favorite *soutzoukakia* [meatballs]."

The reasons for immigrating differed from generation to generation. But while the immigrants had chosen not to live in Greece, most of them shared a desire to still be Greek. They stuck together, forming close-knit communities just as they had in their homeland. Many of them still spoke Greek, especially at home. They still kept their religious traditions and celebrated Greek holidays. They listened to Greek music, watched Greek movies, and danced Greek dances. And of course, they ate Greek food!

Text-Dependent Questions:

1. Why did Greece's currant market suffer in the 1890s?

2. What are padrones?

3. Why did the U.S. change its immigration laws in 1924?

Research Project:

Look up the history of Greek immigration to your area. Is there a notable Greek population now? What organizations help promote Greek culture?

APPETIZER

Before sitting down to the main meal of the day at lunchtime, Greeks often have a glass or two of *ouzo*, a type of Greek liquor that has a licorice-like flavor. To make sure the alcohol doesn't go straight to their head, it's customary to have a plate of *mezedes*, or appetizers, as an accompaniment.

Mezedes are simply small portions of food, and can range from a handful of nuts to a few bites of shrimp or octopus. Variations on staple foods like bread, cheese, and fresh vegetables are the main ingredients in common Greek appetizers.

A classic appetizer is nothing more than a dish of olives, probably Greece's most famous food. In Greek mythology, olives were a gift from the goddess Athena. Raw olives, straight off the tree, taste terrible, but long ago the Greeks figured out how to soak them in brine (salty water) to get rid of the bitter flavor, and then marinate them in vinegar and spices. It's rare today to find a Greek who doesn't like olives. They're an essential part of any Greek's diet, no matter where they live!

Fried cheese, or saganiki, *is another favorite—and extremely easy to make. Slabs of hard cheese are dredged in flour and seared in a small frying pan, and then finished with a squeeze of lemon. For something a little more sophisticated,* spanakopita *packs spinach and cheese between layers of flaky phyllo dough. Cut into small squares, it makes an easy finger food.*

And don't forget the tzatziki, a sauce made from Greek yogurt, slivers of freshly grated cucumber, garlic, salt, and pepper. Bread, zucchini slices, or bites of fried eggplant all get a Greek flair when they're dipped in tzatziki.

Settling In

Hrisanthi spoke only a handful of English words when she **immigrated** to Los Angeles, but back home in Greece, she'd worked for years at a shop, and was certain she could help her husband run his store. She knew how to manage numbers, and she knew how to manage customers, whatever language they spoke. When a dignified gentleman entered the store and ordered a Coca-Cola, she obliged. Back then the drink was mixed at a fountain, combining the Coke syrup with soda water. She made the drink, and gave it to him, and confidently delivered one of her few English phrases: "Ten cents only!" He happily paid the price. Only later did she find out the actual cost was five cents!

Words to Understand

assimilate change oneself to mix better in a new culture

emigrate leave one's home country to live in another country

fasting choosing not to eat for religious or health reasons

immigrated moved into one country from another

menial of low importance and usually high physical difficulty

The all-American soda fountain was one place where Greek Americans could both feel at home but also start to merge with the wider American culture.

New Lives

Despite the occasional mix-up, Hrisanthi was an asset to her husband. Her business skills were just one advantage. More importantly, her arrival now meant that he could start a family.

From 1900 to 1910, only five percent of Greek immigrants were female. There was a huge gender imbalance on both sides of the ocean. Greek men abroad had few potential wives to choose from, and Greek women back home had trouble finding husbands. By the 1920s, however, more women started **emigrating** from Greece, often as picture brides. Although most men had intended to return to Greece, now they changed their plans. They married, started to raise families, and established themselves more per-

Thousands of women from Greece headed to America to find husbands.

manently in their new communities.

It wasn't easy. In the United States, native citizens often had a complicated relationship with immigrants. Many immigrants—no matter where they came from—were considered dirty, lazy, and even dishonest or violent. They were labeled as inferior because they worked **menial** jobs and did not share American customs. Greek immigrants actually were treated better than other groups as a whole, perhaps because Americans respected the ancient Greek culture, with its emphasis on individualism and democracy. But it was still a hard road.

There were also language bar-

Americans had respect for Greek philosophy and history, but not always for Greek immigrants.

riers. Most Greeks spoke little or no English, especially when they first arrived. This closed the door on jobs that required English language skills, and made it more difficult for them to connect with their neighbors. Thelma Siouris was an immigrant who remembered being the only woman in a Utah railroad town. "I was so lonely, I baked cookies and sat on the porch waiting for the school children to come by," she told historian Helen Papanikolas, who wrote several books about Greek immigrants. "I had them sit and eat the cookies and didn't understand what they were saying, but at least I heard the sound of human voices."

Fitting In

Immigrants had different customs, different clothes, and different things in their lunchboxes. In their new countries, all these differences often got lumped under the category of "strange." One Greek child to the United States remembers how he came to school with a lunch of sauteed brains. That was definitely different from the peanut-butter-and-jelly sandwiches of his schoolmates, and earned him some surprised looks. (On the other hand, maybe immigrants thought Americans were the strange ones. Bread stuck together with pulverized nuts? Put that way, it doesn't sound too appetizing!)

Octopus is one of the unusual meals that Greeks enjoy but that Americans might not.

There were efforts by American social organizations to **assimilate** immigrants. Social workers would teach immigrants American ways, from hygiene habits (bathing more often) to proper diet (less sugar). Children were taught to recite the Pledge of Allegiance and sing the U.S. national anthem. Some immigrants tried to fit in, adopting American habits to prove themselves. Others clung to their old ways.

Two cultural organizations were formed to help Greeks in America.

The AHEPA was formed in 1922 to help newly arrived Greek immigrants contact fellow Greeks and find their way in their new home.

One, the Greek American Progressive Association (GAPA) resisted efforts to assimilate Greeks, taking the position that it diluted their national identity. Another, the American Hellenic Educational Progressive Association (AHEPA) took a more lenient approach, urging Greeks to accept American ways even as they preserved their cultural heritage. In the end, AHEPA's efforts were more successful, and as Greeks became more comfortable in their new land, they also started to advance economically.

Nonetheless, they made an effort to keep their heritage alive, and one sure-fire way to do it was to share a meal. The biggest challenge was getting that meal to taste *Greek*.

Greek Foodways

Just as with all people, the Greeks had certain habits surrounding food and meals. These "foodways" had been established for centuries. What they ate—and when and where and why they ate it—was tied to their specific culture, geography, and economic position. Poorer people depended more heavily on bread and vegetables. People who lived on the coasts ate more fish. Throughout Greece, hot food is less common than cold, because the weather is already hot a lot of the time. (When Americans began tasting Greek food for the first time, some complained that it was lukewarm, not realizing that was the way it was supposed to be served.)

Food was also tied closely to religion and holidays. For example, in the Greek Orthodox Church, there are **fasting** days scattered throughout the year. This doesn't mean the Greeks abstain from eating any food at all, but meat is usually off-limits on a fasting day, and sometimes all animal products are forbidden. It's a time of sacrifice, but they make up for it

An Easter Tradition

American children are familiar with the yearly Easter Egg hunt, and "cracking" open plastic eggs to find candy inside. Greek children followed a different tradition. They would hard-boil eggs and dye them red. The color symbolized the blood of Christ, while the egg itself represented the tomb where Christ was buried after his crucifixion. Then, they played a game during which they would hit their eggs together, trying to break their opponent's egg without cracking their own. This was symbolic of Christ emerging from his tomb. Whoever had the shell that lasted the longest, before cracking, was supposed to have good luck.

on holidays, when fasts are broken and the entire community celebrates together in a feast.

Greeks also celebrate their "name day." In the Greek Orthodox Church, every day of the year is earmarked as being the special day for at least one (and sometimes more) saints. People named after that particular saint celebrate on that day. Those with names that are not tied to a saint can celebrate on All Saints Day, which comes about two months after Easter. In Greece, name days are even more important than birthdays.

In America and other countries, Greeks tried to carry on their long-standing traditions, making adjustments to fit their new environment. The food available to them might or might not have been similar to what they could find at home. It varied based on where they lived. In rural or country areas, they might have been able to keep large gardens, or gather

Greek Orthodox churches are often decorated with large paintings, called icons, of saints and other holy people.

wild fruits and greens. In the city, there might have been more access to imported items such as olive oil or feta cheese. But wherever they lived, they learned to adapt their Greek cooking to their new land. Even a small garden could support a few fresh vegetables and some herbs like oregano and dill, which are central in Greek cooking. They also eagerly looked forward to relatives coming over from Greece. Hopefully, they would bring a new stash of olive oil as a gift!

Greek Towns

Slowly, as Greeks became more settled, it became easier to find the foods they liked, especially in urban areas. There, "Greek Towns" spread over several blocks, with businesses that catered just to Greek customers.

As many immigrant groups did, Greeks often lived near other Greeks, establishing neighborhoods that took on the character of their homeland.

 **Eating Healthy**

There's been a lot said in recent years about the healthy Mediterranean diet, of which Greek food is a part. The emphasis is on fresh, simple ingredients, such as tomatoes, olives, bread, and cheese. Artichokes, eggplants, and zucchini turn up in countless meals. Coming from a country almost entirely surrounded by water, Greek food also includes significant amounts of seafood, but meat is much more rare. Although the Greeks were happy to include beef, pork, lamb, and chicken in their dishes if they could, meat was expensive and scarce, and most followed a near-vegetarian diet (except for seafood) out of necessity. Meat was saved for Sundays and special occasions, and recipes often had two versions—one with meat, one without—depending on what was available.

Lowell, Massachusetts, was a town built around cloth mills. Here, one of the first Greek Towns was established. In addition to shoeshine shops, barbers, tailors, and newspapers, there were dozens of businesses focused on food—four restaurants, ten confectioneries (candy stores) and fruit stands, six bakeries, 25 coffeehouses, and 30 general grocery stores! Other Greek Towns emerged in Chicago; Detroit; Astoria, New York; and Tarpon Springs, Florida.

These new "Greek islands" were lifesavers for customers who only spoke Greek, while also offering the specialized products that Greeks craved. Dan Georgakas, a second-generation immigrant raised in Detroit in the 1940s and 1950s, participated in an oral history project conducted by New York's Queens College. He remembers, "You wanted olive oil, you wanted feta, you wanted pastries, you wanted good bread, you wanted good olives—you went to Greek Town, because they didn't have that in the supermarkets."

Even in the sparsely populated West, specialty markets and businesses were established to serve Greeks and other immigrants, selling everything from olives to octopuses. Some enterprising businessmen began raising goats on the outskirts of mill and mining towns, to supply cheese to immigrant homemakers.

The tradition of Greek markets continues, as at this Florida street fair.

Coffee Culture

Another Greek institution that was established early on in America and elsewhere was the *kafenio*, or Greek coffeehouse. Lots of people enjoy a good cup of coffee, and none more so than the Greeks. Never mind that they borrowed the basic recipe from the Turks; Greek coffee is more than a drink, it's a direct line to Greek culture. The kafenio was the place to go.

Small but strong, thick, and black, Greek coffee is usually served in a demitasse (a miniature cup). It's sipped slowly while reading a newspaper or having a conversation, not guzzled out of a Styrofoam cup on the way to work. At the kafenio, men would gather to socialize in their leisure hours, buying a cup of coffee and a Greek pastry as a treat.

It was easy to stay for hours. They read Greek newspapers that brought news of home, smoked cigarettes, played card games, and argued politics. Sometimes there was entertainment, such as a belly dancer, a strong-man,

Inside a Greek cafe in Montreal

A group of musicians performs traditional Greek songs. The mandolin (third from the left) is often a part of Greek music groups.

a mandolin player, or a *karagiozi* (a type of puppet show).

It didn't matter if you were a railroad worker, a storekeeper, a doctor, or unemployed. The kafenio wasn't about class; it was about being Greek. Dan Georgakas remembers, "When you stood on Monroe Street and you looked through the window [of the kafenio], inside was Greece and outside was America."

The division between the two cultures was there, but with each passing year it became fuzzier. Georgakas remembers that his "smorgasbord" neighborhood was home to people from Greece, Ireland, Poland, Italy, and other countries. Children played with each other with little thought to where their parents had been born or what language they spoke. And although Greek families worked to preserve their established traditions, they were also open to new ideas.

Text-Dependent Questions:

1. In the decade between 1900 and 1910, what percentage of Greek immigrants was female?

2. What is a "name day" in Greek culture?

3. What are two reasons Greeks shopped in "Greek Towns"?

Research Project:

Greek Towns are still located all over the United States. Find out more about one. What kinds of businesses are there? What are some of the specialty food products that they sell?

FIRST COURSE

Soup or salad? Both are mainstays in Greek cooking. The key is to use fresh, basic ingredients—beets and beans, tomatoes and potatoes—and give them a Greek flavor with things like capers, feta, or anchovies.

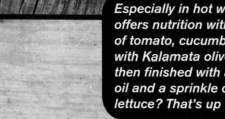

Especially in hot weather, a classic Greek salad offers nutrition without being too heavy. Chunks of tomato, cucumber, and onion are topped with Kalamata olives and hunks of feta cheese, then finished with a drizzle of extra virgin olive oil and a sprinkle of fresh oregano. What, no lettuce? That's up to you—lettuce is optional!

Fassolada—*bean soup*—is one of Greece's national dishes and it's perfect for the colder months. With a base of white beans and tomatoes, it's cheap, easy, nutritious, and tasty. In times of hardship, Greek peasants practically lived on fassolada, since beans were one of the few foods they could find. The basic recipe can also be easily expanded or changed, with various veggies, herbs, and even meat added to taste.

If olives are the king of Greek food, then grapes are the queen. The fruit is used to make wine, while the leaves can be wrapped around a filling to make dolmades. The history of dolmades goes back to ancient wartime, when meat was scarce and creative cooks stretched it by mixing it with seasoned rice and wrapping it in grape leaves. Dolmades can be served hot with a lemony avgolemono sauce, or cold with olive oil.

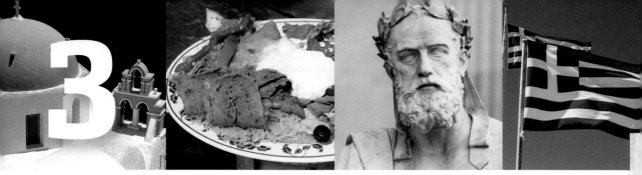

Connecting

Greek immigrants in the late nineteenth and early twentieth centuries mostly shared a common goal. No matter where they went, whether it was America, Australia, Africa, or Europe, the majority of them wanted to return to Greece. In some cases, they did. But over the decades, there was a shift in the minds of many Greeks. Rather than feeling displaced from their native country and homesick to return, they gradually came to accept their new country as home. They made friends in their new home. They brought over relatives to join them. They had homes and jobs. They were learning to speak a new language. And hard times in Greece weren't over. Why go back?

Of course, it did not happen overnight. Instead, as new generations became more comfortable in their adopted land, they were more able to appreciate all it had

Words to Understand

boisterous   loud, raucous, and enthusiastic
niche   a small cleft or nook; an empty place to be filled
repartee   humorous casual talk

At this Greek festival in Canada, a young Greek immigrant hands out flags of her native land to her new friends and neighbors.

to offer. Especially compared to the hardships faced by their family and friends back in Greece, immigrants were often much better off economically. Celeste Theofilos recalls that her parents remembered Greece fondly, but adds, "It was never even a consideration to move back." In their New York home in the middle of the twentieth century, they fit in and enjoyed financial success. In Greece, "they [went] through wars, through famine. [Here] it was very comfortable, and they assimilated very well."

At any Greek festival, roasting meat is always a popular part of the street food, such as here in Florida.

Putting Down Roots

Church was central to the lives of many Greek immigrants. While Americans practiced many different religions, Greeks were united in that almost all belonged to the Greek Orthodox Church, a form of Christianity. For early immigrants, establishing churches in their new homes was a high priority. The church was a place to worship, but it also served a key social function.

Though located in Colorado, St. John's Greek Orthodox proudly uses Greek letters.

Through church-sponsored festivals and picnics, Greek immigrants raised money to send to their relatives back home, or to use for a needed service in their new community. Everyone chipped in to cover the costs of food, entertainment—and a little bit extra.

Events such as these also helped introduce Greeks to the larger community. Greek immigrants were close-knit, but they were not introverted or exclusive. In fact, they were known for being demonstrative and emotional. They enjoyed **boisterous** dancing and loud music. When word got out about the fun, other people began showing up and were introduced to Greek customs, culture, and food.

Children got an extra dose of Greek culture by attending Greek schools. Parents wanted to make sure their children learned the Greek language and Greek traditions, so they formed special schools for their children to attend. After going to regular public school for most of the day, Greek children got a little break and then reported to "Greek school" for another two hours in the evening. Students usually started around age 7 or 8 and quit when they went to high school. Some kids joked that it was like reform school, because the teachers were so strict. "The teachers had little pity on us," writes second-generation immigrant Nick Thomopoulos in his

Candy and soda fountain counters like this one were located all over Chicago in the early 1900s, and many were run by Greek-Americans.

Sweet Tooth

You don't hear much about Russian tacos or German pizza or pumpkin pie from Japan. Two centuries ago, you didn't hear much about Greek candy, either. The Greeks were known for cookies and pastries, but they weren't big on candy-making. Greek immigrants to America changed that. Seeing that Americans had an insatiable sweet tooth, the Greeks adapted their baking skills into making candy—which was actually easier and more profitable than labor-intensive pastries.

By 1918, Chicago, Illinois, had become the country's confectionery capital, with Greeks at the helm of some 6,000 candy and ice cream shops. They spread across the country from there. Candy stores went hand-in-hand with another business that attracted Greek immigrants: movie theaters. In fact, one Greek confectioner from St. Louis remembered being invited by two brothers, also Greek immigrants, to join them in opening a theater. He turned them down and offered a piece of advice: "Stay in the candy business!" (They didn't listen—and eventually went on to become the heads of major movie studios!)

book *100 Years: From Greece to Chicago and Back*. "If we ditched school, the teachers could easily find out, and we would suffer the next day both at school and at home."

Moving Up the Ladder

Be your own boss. That's an attractive idea to a lot of people, and Greek immigrants in particular showed an entrepreneurial spirit. Although they may have had to start in low-paying jobs working for an employer, as soon as they could, they went into business for themselves.

Greek-owned businesses were largely family affairs. While the immigrants worked their way up the economic ladder, saving their money, they kept watch for opportunities to either start a business or take over an existing one. The capital needed to invest in a business could be substantial, so it was typical for them to partner with another family member in the community. That way, they would share both the risk and the work.

The story of George Menzelos' grandfather, who arrived in 1904, is typical. He came over to join family members who had already settled in the United States. Over the years, "he saved money and invested in a partnership in a grocery store," says Menzelos. "Then he saved more money and

The long tradition of food and hospitality of the Greek coffee house migrated to America and soon many large cities had Greek cafes.

he invested in another grocery store. And eventually he bought one."

The restaurant business was an especially big draw for Greek immigrants. At one point in the early part of the century, it was estimated that roughly a third of all urban restaurants in the Northeast were operated by Greeks. Again, the reason was tied to the Industrial Revolution.

At the turn of the twentieth century, mills and factories were changing the landscape of cities

Xenia

You never know what the gods are up to. Ancient Greeks believed that the gods might send poor beggars to their door—or even disguise themselves as one—as a test to see whether the residents would offer charity. Selfish or distrustful people who turned them away might pay for their mistake later, when the gods punished them. The smart ones practiced xenia, or hospitality, welcoming any and all comers. Whether or not the gods were really at work, it was important to extend hospitality and friendship to friends and strangers alike. Especially in olden times, there were fewer places people could seek food and shelter during their travels, so they depended on private citizens. Greek immigrants continued this practice in their new countries, opening their homes to visitors and serving them a good meal. It was best to show up hungry—guests who did not eat might offend their hosts!

in America, Britain, and Australia. Hundreds or even thousands of workers crowded into a relatively small space to work the machines. Sometimes they were given a break for lunch or dinner (and sometimes not). But whenever they did get the chance to eat, they needed something quick and inexpensive. Greek immigrants quickly saw a **niche**. They set up food carts on the streets, and opened diners and luncheonettes near the factories, where workers could grab a bite.

Of course, they did not just serve Greek food—in fact, they may not

Tom's was a famous diner in Brooklyn, New York, run by a Greek-American who became a local hero.

have served their native dishes at all. Instead, they learned to cook American favorites, such as roast turkey, meat loaf, hot dogs, corned beef and cabbage (an Irish import), or pizza (an Italian import).

But the Greek ambiance was always in the background. Barbara Aliprantis, a Greek immigrant who grew up in Brooklyn, New York, wrote in a 2016 blog post about her father, "When he arrived at work, Anastasios transformed into 'Tom,' a proud new-American, proprietor of a Greek Coffee Shop—American Style! He'd joke unabashedly with the customers in his broken English and serve up the 'blue plate specials' with a big smile on his face, steady banter and amusing **repartee**! The customers loved him!"

A Taste of Home

Immigrants catered to American tastes in their restaurants, but at home they worked hard to make Greek food part of their daily meals—and part of their children's memories. Ruth Bardis' parents moved to Australia in the middle of the twentieth century. "We didn't eat in our home just to sustain our day; rather, eating was a lifestyle," she writes in her book *Memories Made in a Greek Kitchen*. "There is a Greek saying: 'One is born around the family table, and one dies around the family table.'"

What they ate wasn't fancy, but it was healthy and wholesome. Bardis' parents' families had grown up poor in Greece, with a diet based on vegetables. Once they moved to Australia, they kept the focus on eating local food, but there was one import that got some shelf space in their home: Attica honey, which comes from bees that feed on thyme plants in Greece. "My parents would oblige us to eat a spoonful a day with a handful of nuts," Bardis writes. "Dad insisted this was our form of natural antibiotics!"

History of Greek cafes

Mizithra is a soft Greek cheese that can be shaved and put on food.

Growing up half a world away in Los Angeles, George Menzelos remembers a multi-ethnic table. It was part Greek, and part American. In his home, Sunday afternoons meant getting the whole extended family together to grill a lamb riblet, a favorite food in Greece. "It was 39 cents a pound. My mom said she could feed 40 people with that," says Menzelos. "That's not to say my mom once a week didn't make mac and cheese or barbecue, or hamburgers and hot dogs, or that we wouldn't go out and order a pizza. But most of the cooking was done in the Greek style."

That could be good and bad. One of his childhood memories is of his grandmother making a certain pasta dish that was topped with mizithra, a type of cheese made from sheep's or goat's milk. Served fresh, mizithra has a mild taste, but Menzelos remembers that it was imported from Greece, a trip that could take several months on a ship. By the time it arrived, "It was just old and smelly, nothing like you experience today," he remembers. "To Greeks, they want that nostalgic flavor. To me, it was poison!"

Text-Dependent Questions:

1. When did children attend Greek school?

2. Many Greeks started their own businesses. What was one of the most popular kinds?

3. According to legend, why do Greeks practice *xenia*?

Research Project:

Greeks liked to keep up on current events. Whether they were socializing at the kafenio or just relaxing at home, one popular activity was reading the newspaper! The Greek press was very active in the early part of the century; some papers were published in Greek, and some in English. Find out more about the Greek press now. What issues do they cover?

SECOND COURSE

A good Greek cook knows how to roast a lamb and grill an octopus (the little ones, not the big ones!), but for everyday cooking, the bulk of a Greek meal is built around vegetables, starches, legumes, and dairy products. Regular food meant soups, stews, and casseroles—all made with local food that was in season.

When Greek immigrants began to spread across the globe, there were more challenges in re-creating favorite foods. Some basic ingredients, like potatoes or beans, were relatively easy to find. Others, like eggplants, olives, or feta cheese, might only be stocked at a specialty market. But with a jar of olive oil, a bottle of red wine vinegar, a few lemons and some thyme and oregano, even unfamiliar foods could be transformed into new versions of Greek favorites.

Moussaka is probably the best known of all Greek dishes, and probably originated when nearby Arab cultures brought the eggplant to Greece. Moussaka combines layers of sliced eggplant (and sometimes potatoes), minced meat such as beef or lamb, and a milk-and-egg custard. Cheese on top finishes the dish, and moussaka is the perfect place to use authentic Greek cheeses like kefalotiri, a hard cheese made from the milk of sheep or goats.

SOUVLAKI

CHICKEN
LAMB
FALAFEL
BEEF

COMBO

PLATTERS

DIMITRIS GREEK FOOD

@letsnomnom

Street vendors selling souvlaki are a common sight in Greece, and by the early twentieth century they were popping up in places all over the world as Greek immigrants settled abroad. Sometimes called the "fast food" of Greece, souvlaki is an easy meal that combines chunks of marinated and broiled meat with vegetables and tsatziki sauce, then wraps it all up in a pita pocket so it's easy to handle on the go.

SECOND COURSE

With more than 13,000 miles of coastline, Greece is a country with a long history of seafaring—and sea-eating. Fish is a standby, but because big fish are usually more expensive, the Greek diet also includes a lot of smaller fish like sardines and anchovies. (As a bonus, they're also healthier!) Other sea creatures—octopus, calamari (squid), mussels, and shrimp—all make the menu, too. A classic Greek recipe is for kakavia, or fish stew. Named for the pot the ancient Greeks used to cook it in, kakavia is a versatile recipe, using whatever fish, seafood, or veggies are available. If you want to be really authentic, leave the fish heads on while making the broth, to get the best flavor.

For orthodox Greeks, Easter is the year's most important holiday. Many people attend church every day the week before. They also fast to remember the suffering of Christ. But when Easter Sunday comes, it's a day for celebration—and fasting turns to feasting. The traditional main course is roast lamb, chosen because of its significance in the Bible, and a side of roasted potatoes. Traditionally, the lamb is cooked over an open fire, turning it on a spit, but it's okay to be modern and just roast it in the oven, too!

Reaching Back

Since the first big push of immigration began in the late 1800s, Greeks have spread all over the world. The Greek culture they brought with them changed as they started lives in new places. Today, being "Greek" can mean being Greek-Greek, Greek-American, Greek-Australian, or any number of other variations.

Changing Times

Today's third- and fourth-generation immigrants have different priorities than their ancestors.

As a teenager in the 1970s, George Menzelos discovered he had a big interest in food. He got his two Greek grandmothers to teach him how to cook, and then he announced to his family that he wanted to be a chef. "They were horrified!" he remembers. "They said, 'No, you can't do that. Those are the kinds of jobs that our

Words to Understand

dollop a small amount

The Greek salad is a well-known variation on a classic dish, gathering together the fruits and vegetables of Greece, and featuring black olives.

immigrant parents did, because they *had* to. You're going to university to get a degree.'"

A quarter of a century later, attitudes had changed. Marianna Leivadi-taki remembers moving from the Greek island of Crete to England in 2000. She was a psychology student, but she always loved food. At home, she had grown up eating fresh-caught fish every day. She knew how to hang octopuses on a clothesline to dry them out before cooking. Those kinds of things were foreign in England. "I arrived in a country I hardly knew anything about. The culture here is different. The way people are with one another is different. The way people eat is extremely different!" But

The Shish Kebab and the Gyro

A *shish kebab*, with alternating chunks of meat and vegetables, skewered on a stick and cooked to perfection, is a classic Greek food. Then again, so is the gyro—a giant envelope of pita bread stuffed full of roasted meat, chopped tomatoes and onions, and a generous dollop of tzatziki sauce. The kebab keeps each bite carefully separated, to be savored individually, the gyro lumps everything together. Different generations of Greek immigrants to America have been compared to these two staples of Greek cuisine. Earlier immigrants took the kebab approach. They remained somewhat apart in their new lands, keeping Greek customs separate from American ones. In the privacy of their own homes, they remained fully "Greek," while in public or at work, they embraced American ways. Later generations were more like gyros. They combined Greek and American customs to make new traditions that represented the best of both.

Making a Greek salad

Leivaditaki took those differences and turned them into a career. She became a chef, and now she makes Greek dishes every day.

Leivaditaki goes back to Crete whenever she can, but she also works to maintain her Greek heritage in London. "I think that keeping your Greek heritage is so much easier than allowing it to fade away. The second is almost impossible," she says. "The re-creation of events similar to what you are used to, whether it's large gatherings fueled with lots of food and gossiping or playing your favorite Greek songs really loud and having a dance is what brings home closer."

Combining Cultures

Add a dash of ingenuity and a **dollop** of time, and mix thoroughly. That's the basic recipe for how Greek immigrant cooking evolved. Adaptation was key to every aspect of immigrant life, and it started over the kitchen stove.

In the 1950s, Betty Crocker was as American as, well, apple pie. Betty wasn't actually a real person—she was invented by a food company to put a homey face on their products and encourage American families to buy them. Her signature red-and-white cookbook was on the shelf of millions of homes and generations grew up eating her recipes, no matter if they were born in America or somewhere else. Menzelos' mother was Greek, but her cooking definitely had a U.S. influence. In fact, Menzelos called her "Betty Crockopoulos," giving a Greek spin to the American name.

In his home, it was common for American ingredients to creep into traditional recipes. One traditional Easter treat is called *koulourakia*, a butter cookie that's twisted up and then baked. Menzelos had been eating them his whole life. At one point he became curious about the actual recipe,

Small sesame seeds often decorate the holiday cookies known as koulourakia.

and dug it up. "I assumed they had olive oil," he says. "Lo and behold, the recipe calls for Crisco." Menzelos' grandmother also gave an American twist to the classic Greek dessert, *baklava*. It's traditionally made with honey and nuts layered between thin sheets of *phyllo* [FEE-loh] dough, but his grandmother adapted the recipe to add a pumpkin filling. It made a perfect dish for a Greek-American Thanksgiving!

Koumbari

It's common in Western cultures to have a best man or maid of honor at a wedding. This person is the main support system for the bride or groom. It's also traditional, especially in religious families, to have godparents who assume the responsibility of helping to take care of a child. In Greece, these functions are taken on by the *koumbaros* (male) or *koumbara* (female). These are usually longtime, close friends of a couple, and the relationships last a lifetime. Even if they are not blood relatives, the koumbari become just like family for practical purposes. They're invited to family gatherings, and can be an important part of a family's business, just as an uncle or cousin would. For Greek immigrants, it was both regular family and koumbari that helped them establish strong family ties in their new countries.

Sometimes certain ingredients aren't available, and it's necessary to find a substitute. Sometimes it's important to add in a favorite new ingredient (like pumpkin). It's just tradition with a twist.

Staying in Touch

Compared to a century—or even a quarter century—ago, it's much easier for Greeks all over the world to connect with friends or family. In the past, relatives depended on letters that took weeks to cross the ocean, and could easily get lost. Happenings in the family or community were old news by the time they heard about them. Returning home for a wedding or funeral

As in many families, traditions are passed down in Greek households starting at the dinner table.

was not practical. In the best-case scenario, a man could send for his wife and children, who had stayed behind in Greece, and bring them to live with him. But extended families saw each other rarely; some, once they parted, never saw each other again.

It's hard to imagine how difficult that would be in today's world, where people use technology to stay in touch. Greeks today hold regular phone calls, exchange emails, and use Skype to see the faces of loved ones. Returning to Greece every few years is also a priority, and "the trip" is a well-established event in the Greek community. Family bonds are tight, and loyalty lasts for generations. Early emigrants left Greece to help their families, and the people who remained behind never forgot that help.

Today, the children and grandchildren of immigrants share the task that their ancestors began years ago. Just like their parents and grand-parents, they're working to keep Greek traditions strong and vibrant. It's not just about coming together at holidays and weddings, Sunday dinners and weekend picnics. It's about laughing at family stories over a simple Tuesday breakfast, or sharing a coffee after work. Their heritage was born in Greece, but what keeps it alive are the things they do every day, wherever they live.

Text-Dependent Questions:

1. Why did George Menzelos' parents not want him to become a chef?

2. How were the shish kebab and the gyro compared to immigrant life?

3. How did George Menzelos' grandmother make her baklava suitable for an American Thanksgiving?

Research Project:

Plan your own Greek feast! Decide whom you'll invite, and what dishes you want to serve. Then, find recipes for everything. Next, determine where you'll need to shop to get some of the more exotic ingredients. If you're ambitious, get a friend to help you and start cooking!

DESSERT

No dessert until you eat your dinner! Most kids in America have heard that at least once, but it's not as common in Greek families. They don't save their sweets for after dinner. Instead, they're more likely to enjoy cakes and cookies with a cup of strong coffee or a glass of milk in the afternoon.

The Greeks didn't invent the classic pastry baklava, *but it was very early Greek immigrants—sailors who traveled to Mesopotamia in the third century BCE—who discovered it was delicious and snapped up all they could get. While they were at it, they snagged the recipe. Greek cooks revised the recipe by rolling the pastry into flaky, paper-thin sheets of phyllo dough before layering them with honey, walnuts, and pistachios. Then they baked it and finished up with more honey poured on top and left to soak in. Don't expect to whip up a batch of baklava in 30 minutes. Traditionally, Greeks spent hours at the task, carefully stacking 33 layers of phyllo and filling—one for each year in the life of Christ.*

Everyone can use a little luck, so it's unlikely that anyone will turn down a piece of the vasilopita *cake on New Year's Day. This simple white cake—flour, butter, and sugar—is often flavored with lemon or orange, and sometimes a touch of almond extract. But there's another secret "ingredient"—a coin baked inside. When it's ready, the oldest member of the household cuts the cake and gives a piece to everyone in the house, guests included. Whoever gets the piece with the coin is set to have good luck all year. The tradition can be traced to Saint Basil, who is said to have baked his money into small pies and distributed it to the poor.*

Dolmades:

Ingredients:
*   2.2 pounds fatty ground beef (raw)*
*   1 large onion, chopped*
*   ¼ cup flat-leaf parsley, finely chopped*
*   1 teaspoon each of salt and pepper*
*   1/2 cup long-grain white rice, or more to taste*
*   Grape leaves*

Preparation:
Combine first five ingredients, sprinkle with cold water, and mash together. Wrap filling with the grape leaves.

In a 3–4 quart pot, place broken or leftover grape leaves on the bottom, and stack the dolmades on top of the leaves in layers.

Place a heavy, heat-resistant plate on top of the dolmades to hold them in place.

Cover with hot water, 4 teaspoons of olive oil, and salt and pepper.

Simmer on low heat for one hour, adding water when necessary to keep the dolmades covered.

Yield: 40-60 dolmades

Find Out More

Books

Ingram, W. Scott. *Greek Immigrants*. New York: Facts on File, 2004.

Villios, Lynne. *Cooking the Greek Way*. Minneapolis: Lerner Publications, 2002.

Web Sites:

http://www.everyculture.com/multi/Du-Ha/Greek-Americans.html
Learn about when and why Greeks came to America, and the customs they brought with them.

https://www.libertyellisfoundation.org/immigration-museum
Most Greek immigrants came to America through Ellis Island in New York. Find out more about immigration to America here, and even research your own history!

https://myimmigrationstory.com/
It's not just Greek immigrants that have contributed to America's rich culture. Read personal stories about immigrants from all over the world at this site.

http://greek.food.com/
Get inspiration here for cooking the Greek way!

Series Glossary of Key Terms

acclimate to get used to something

assimilate become part of a different society, country, or group

bigotry the practice of treating the members of a racial or ethnic group with hatred and intolerance

culinary having to do with the preparing of food

diaspora a group of people who live outside the area in which they had lived for a long time or in which their ancestors lived

emigrate leave one's home country to live in another country

exodus a mass departure of people from one place to another

first-generation American someone born in the U.S. whose parents were foreign-born

immigrants those who enter another country intending to stay permanently

naturalize become established as though you were native; to gain the rights and privileges of citizenship

oppression a system of forcing people to follow rules or a system that restricts freedoms

presentation in this series, meaning the style in which food is plated and served

Index

Photo Credits

About the Author

Diane Bailey has written more than 50 nonfiction books for kids and teens, on topics ranging from science to sports to celebrities. She also works as a freelance editor, helping authors who write novels for children and young adults. Diane has two sons and two dogs, and lives in Kansas.